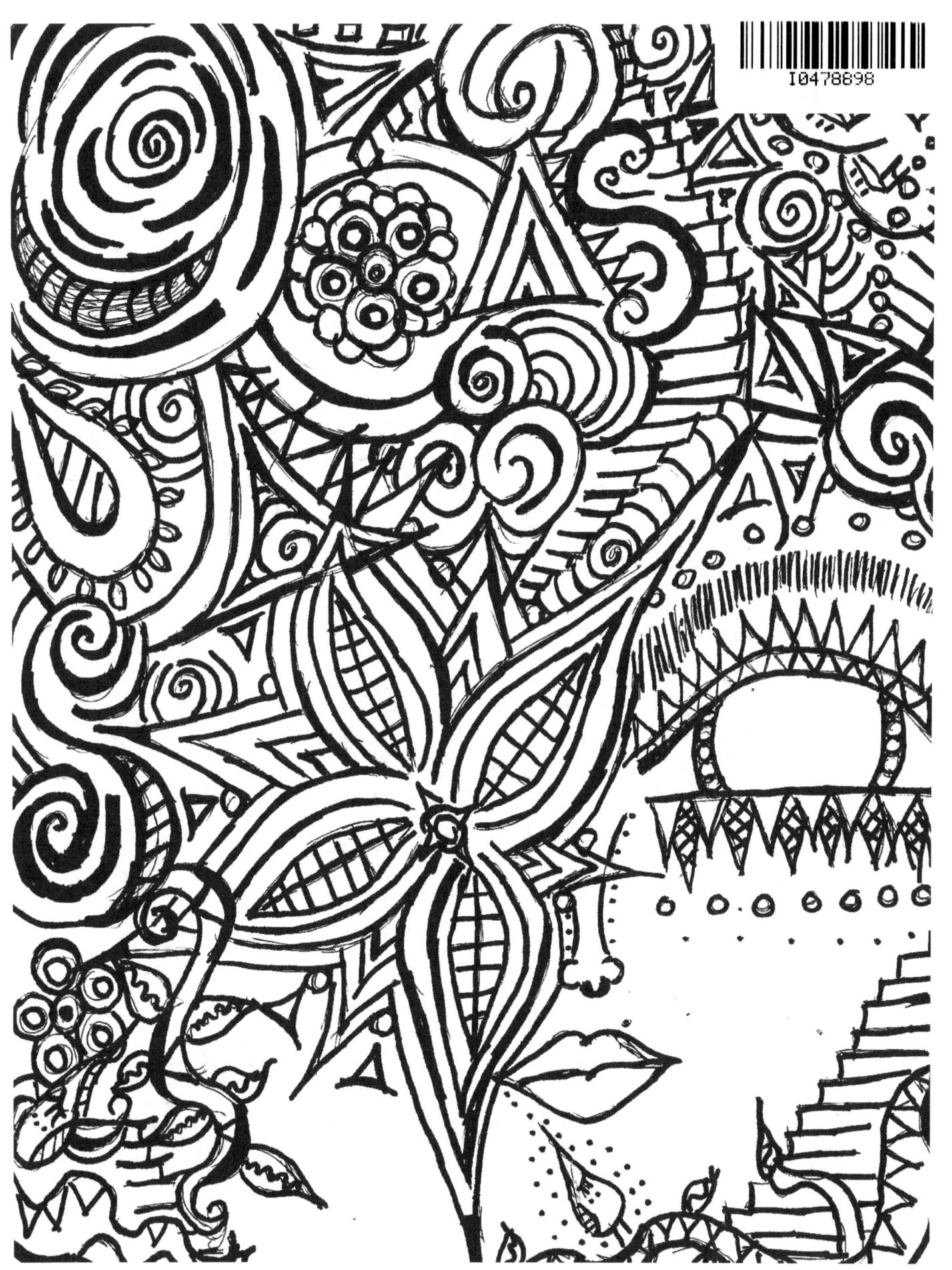

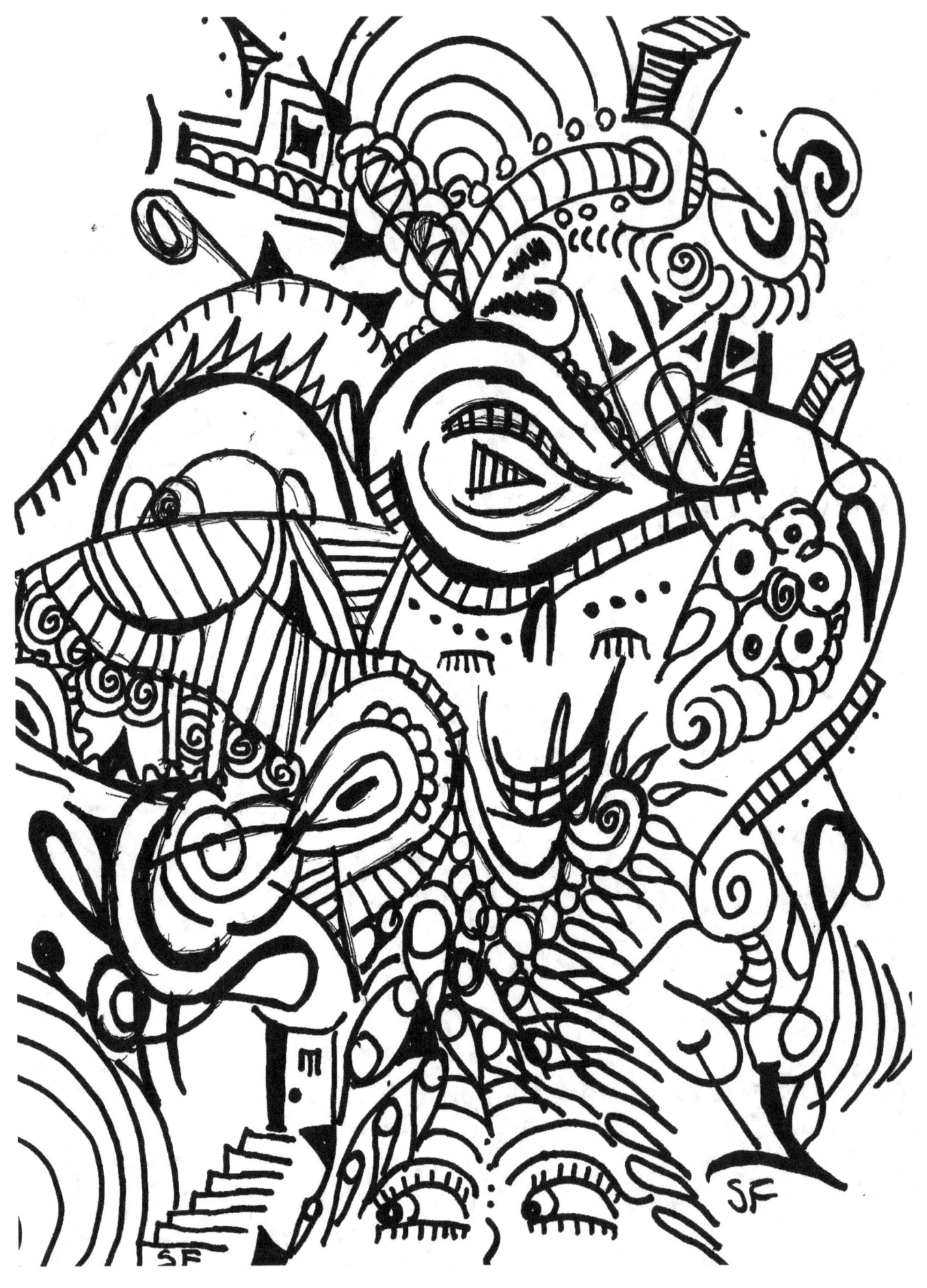

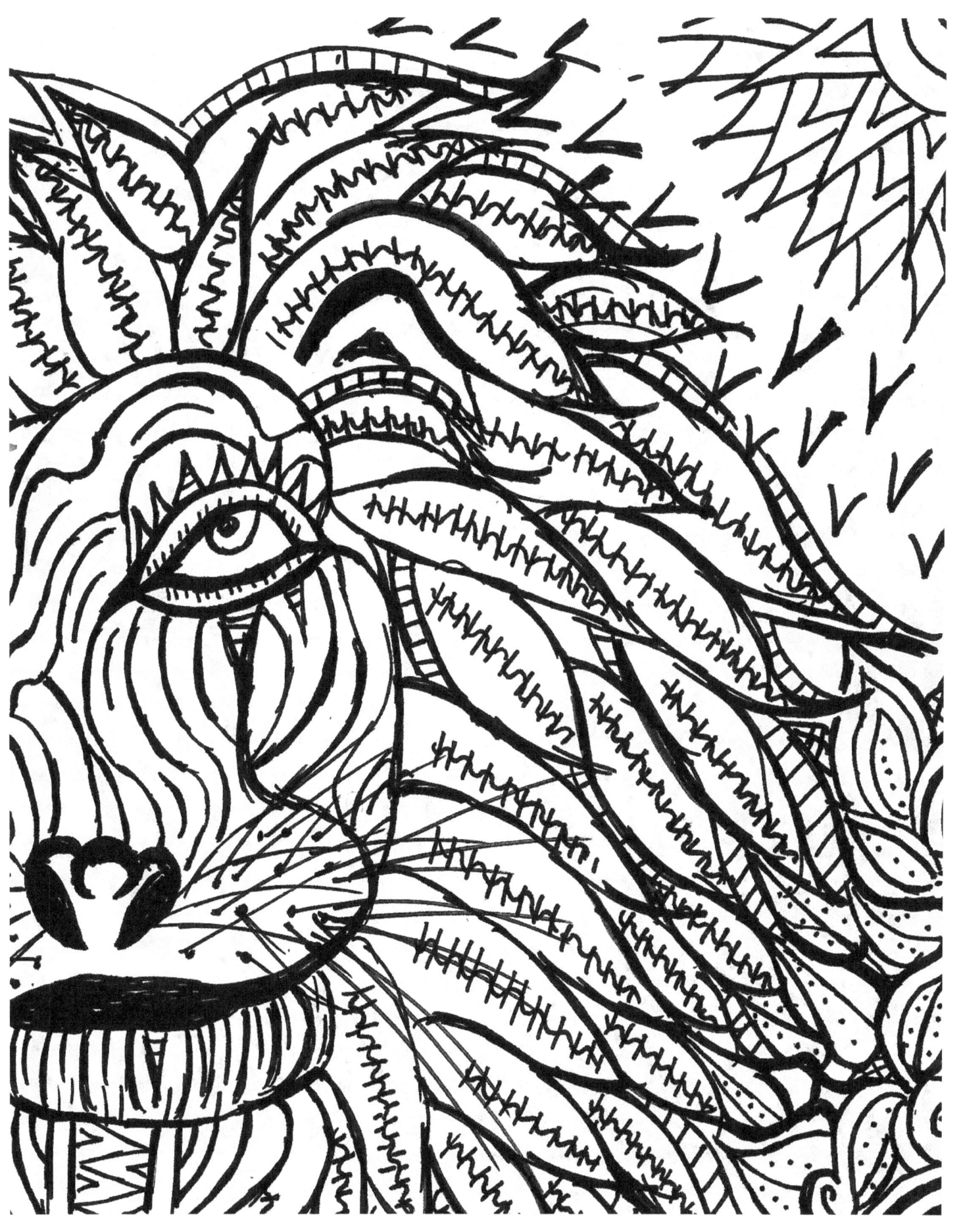

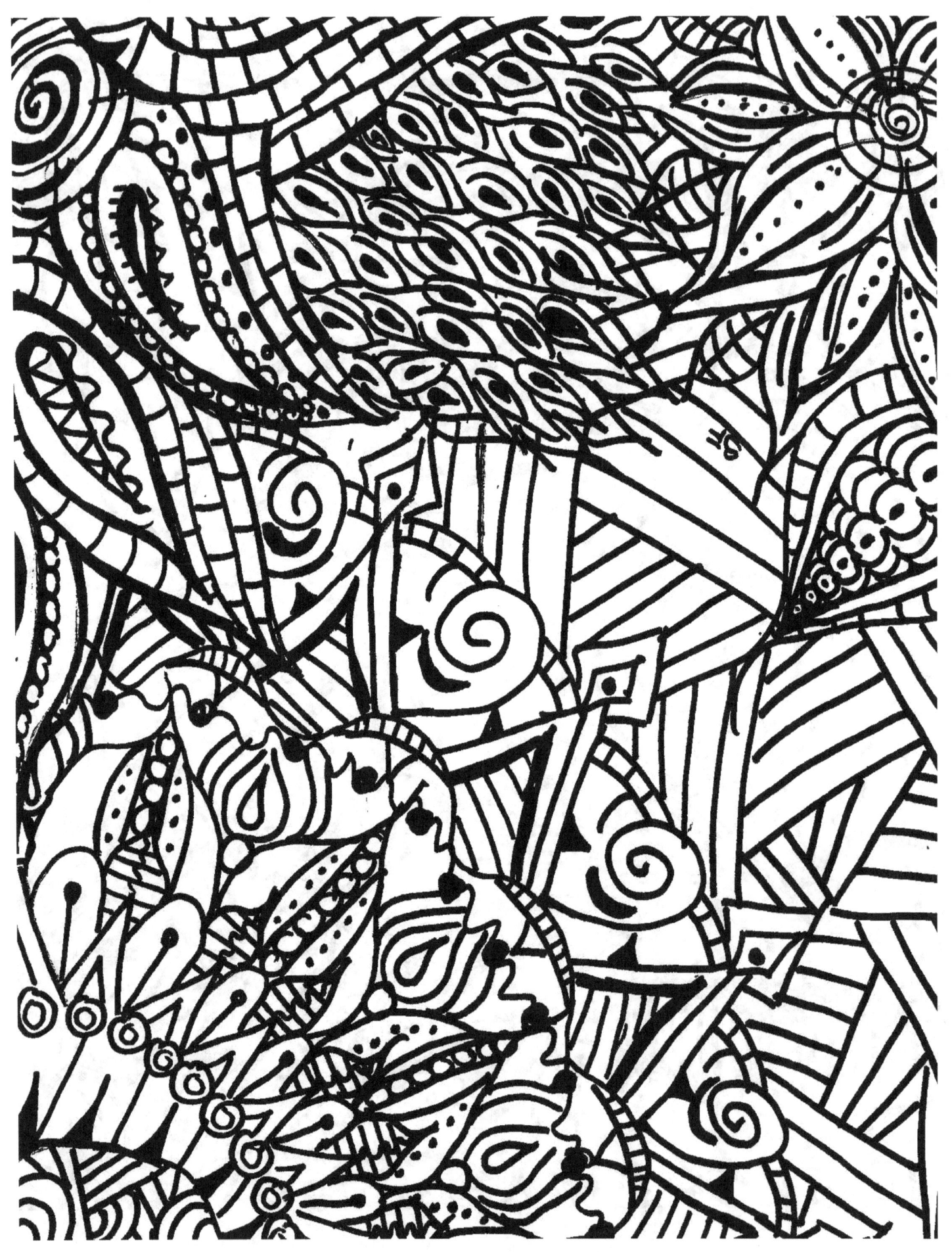

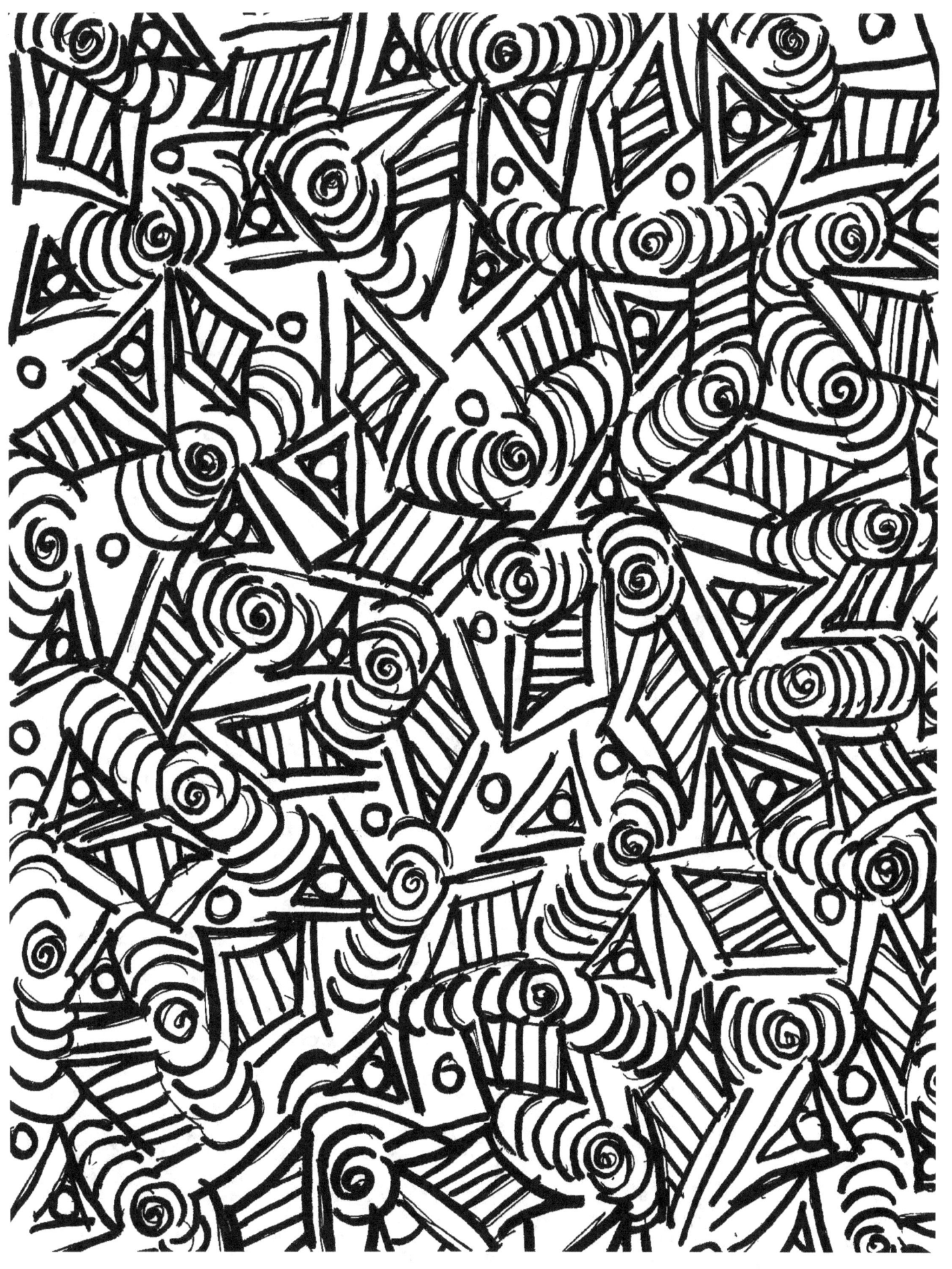

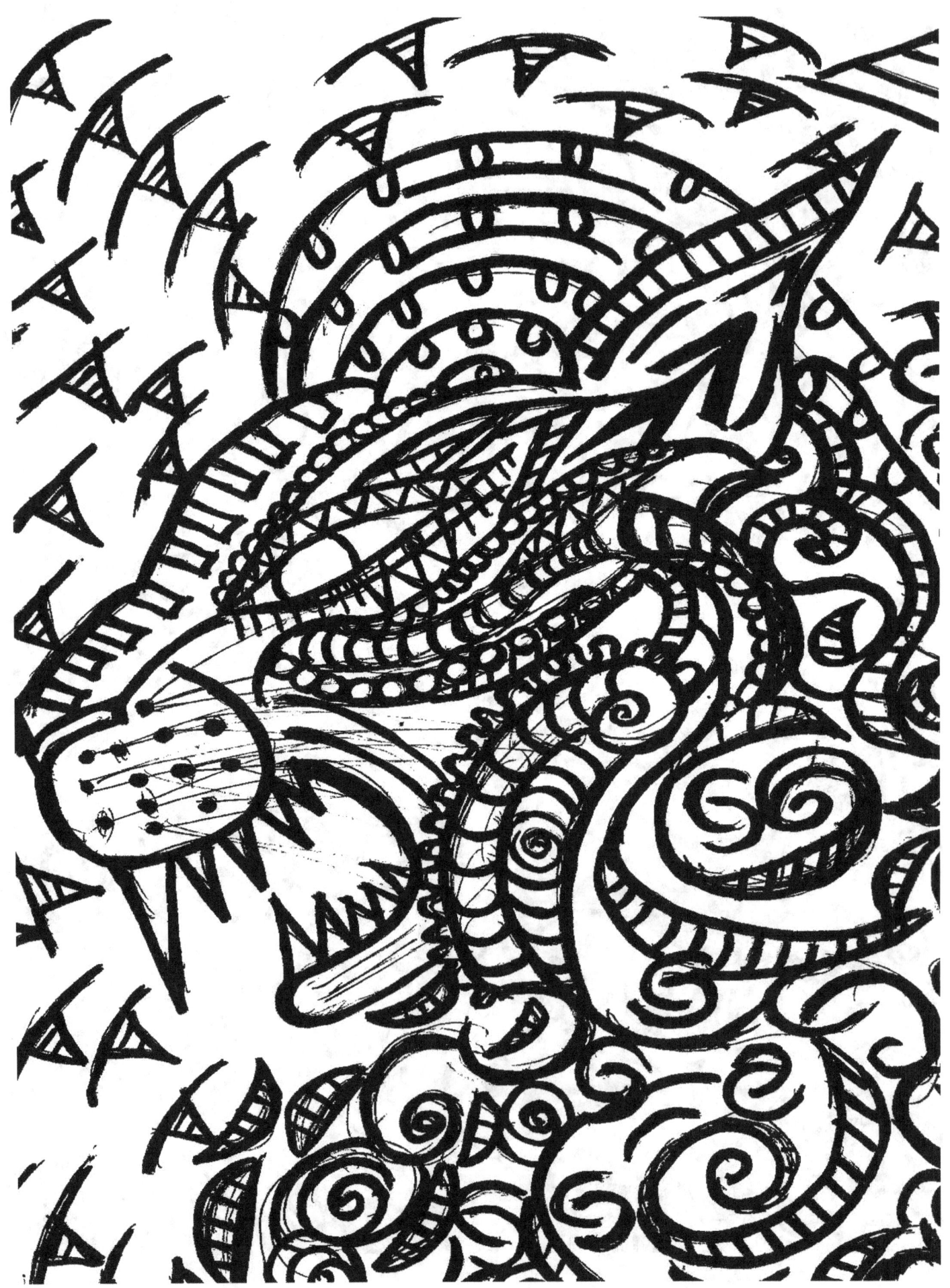

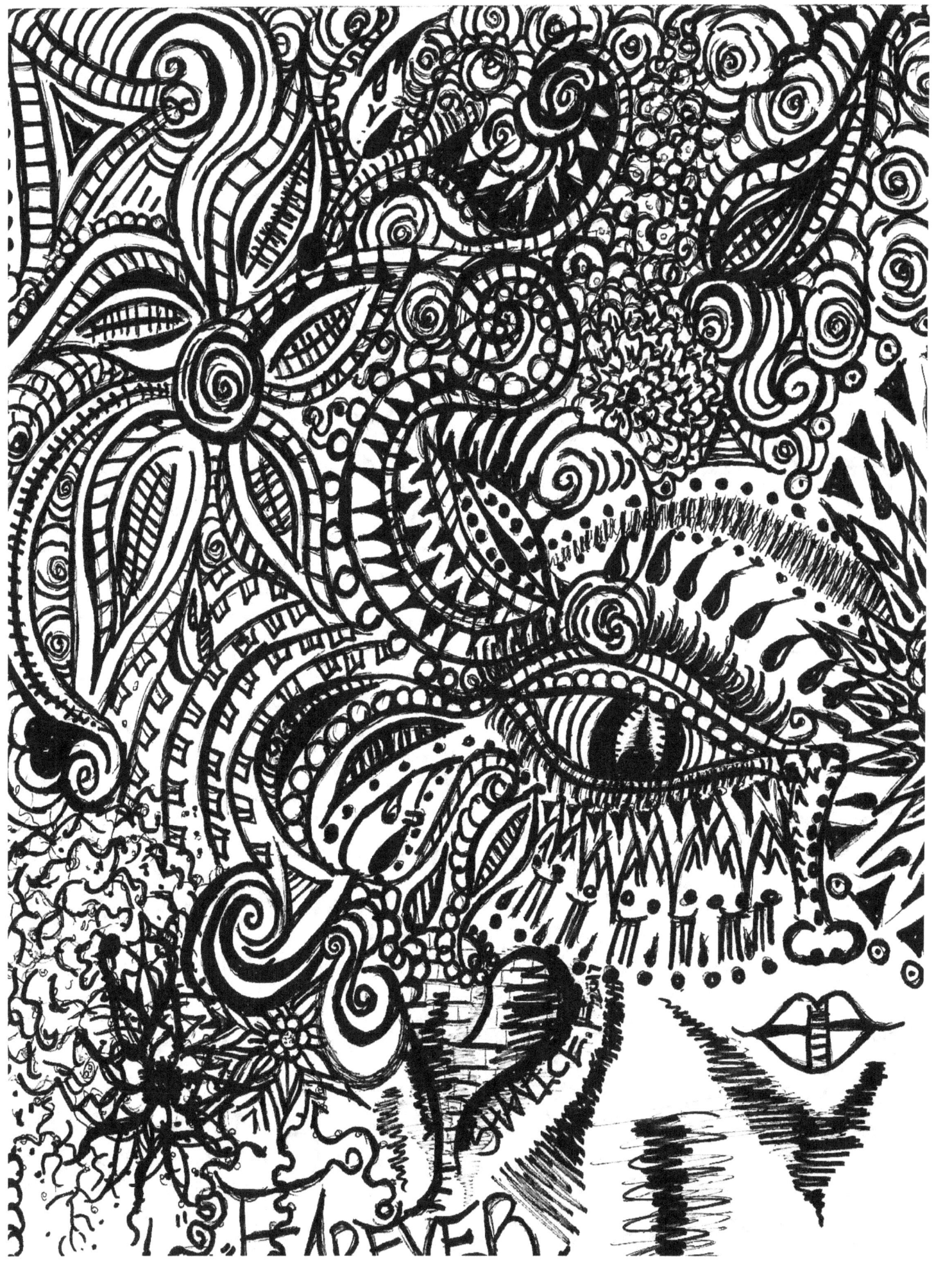

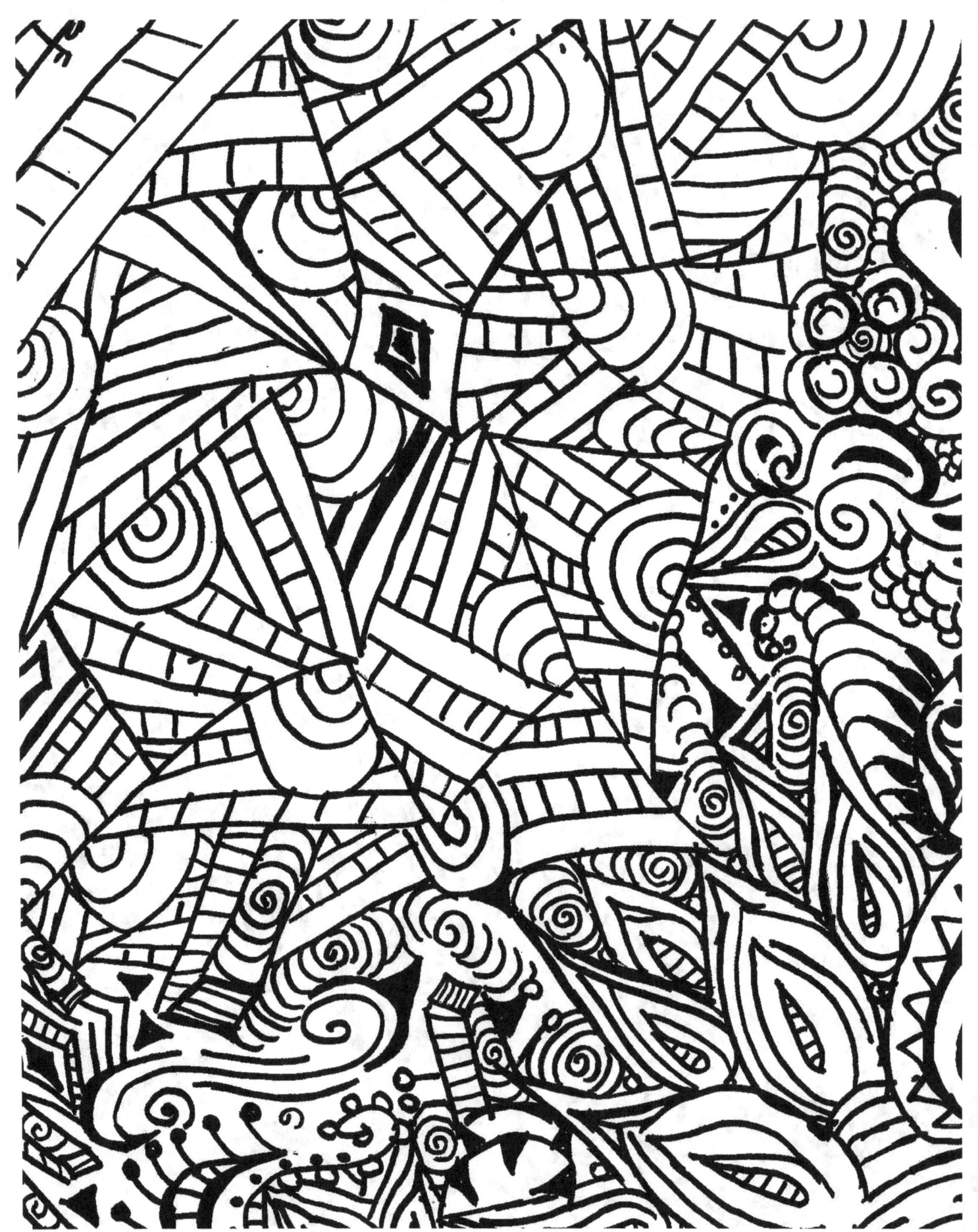

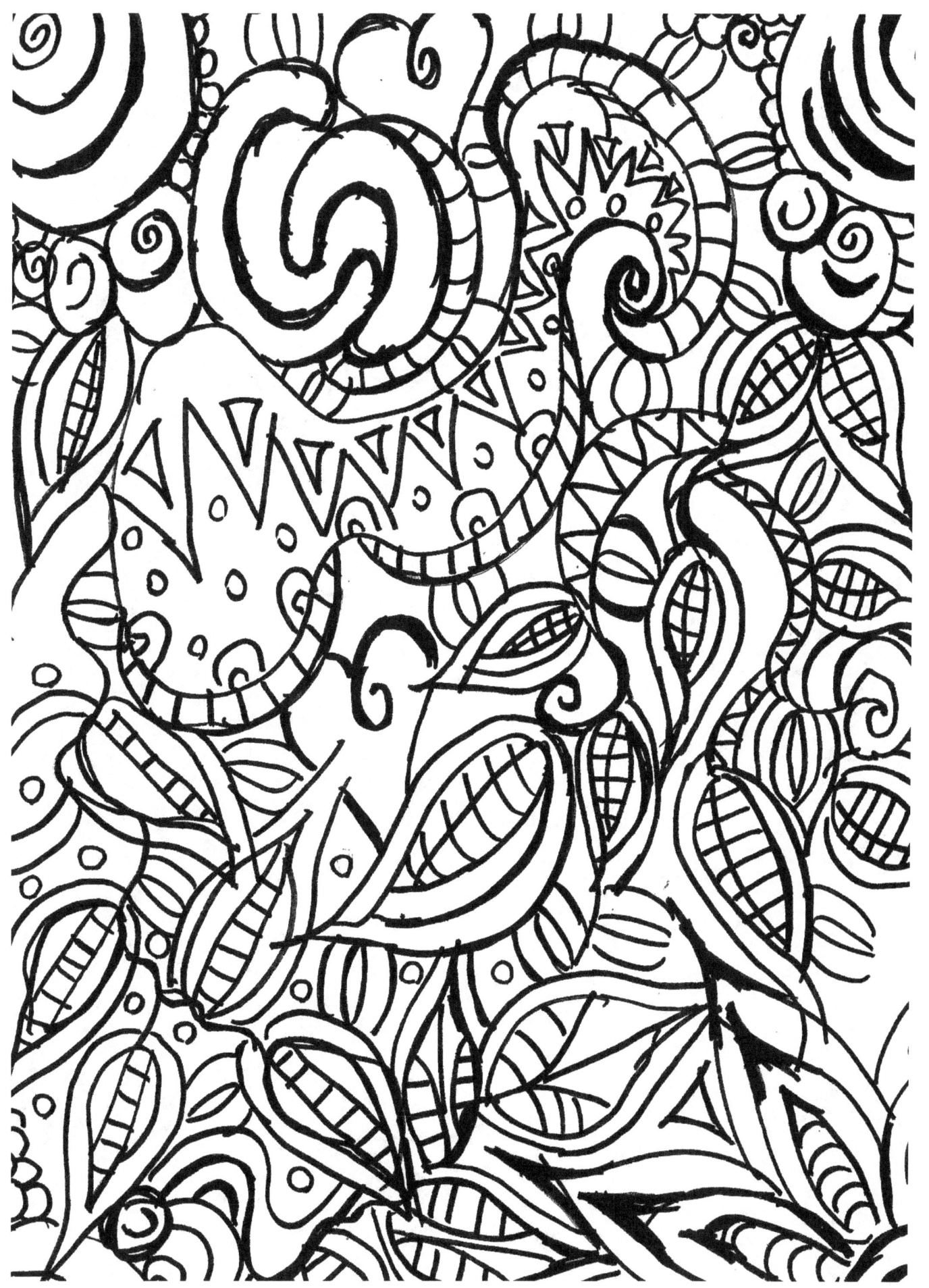

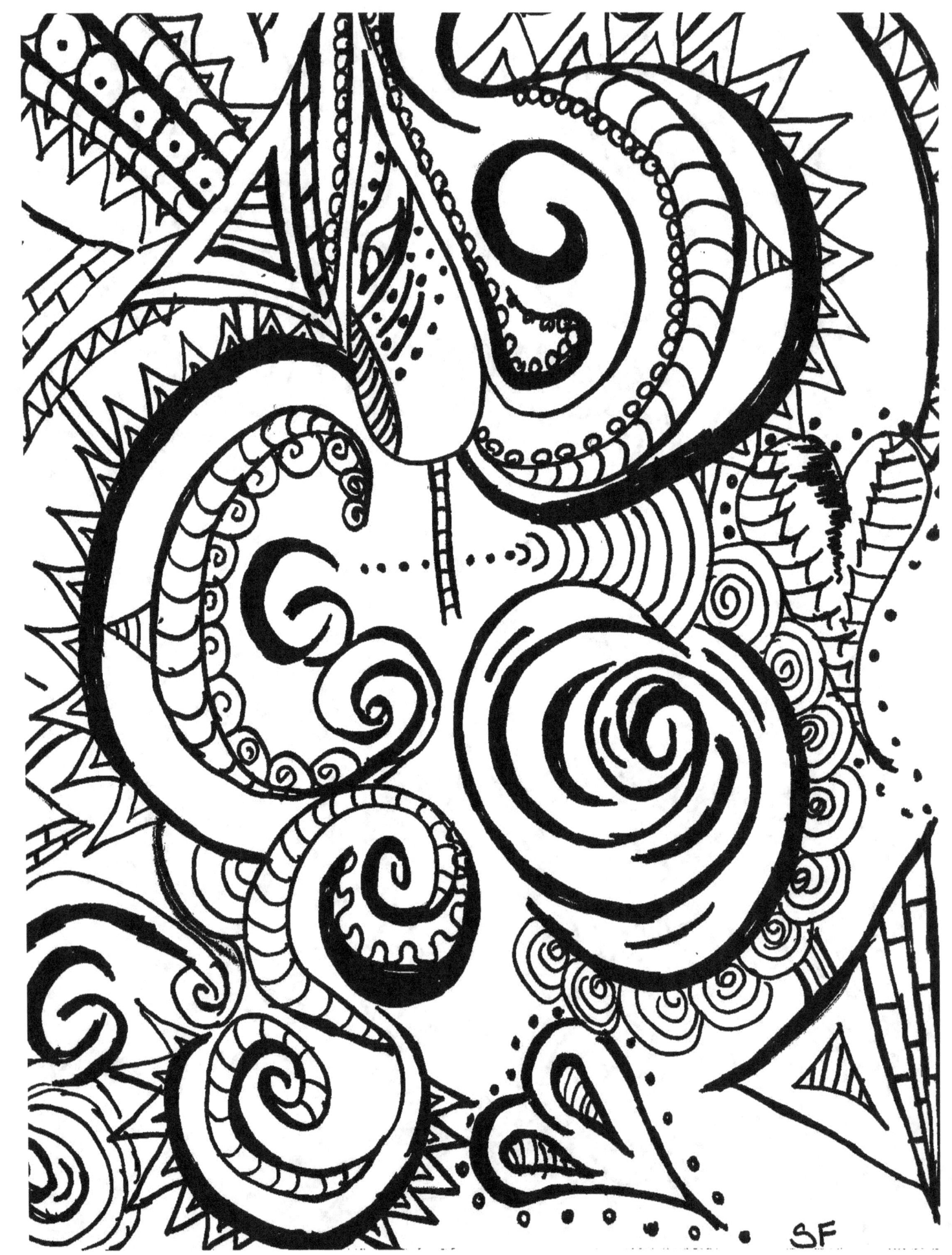

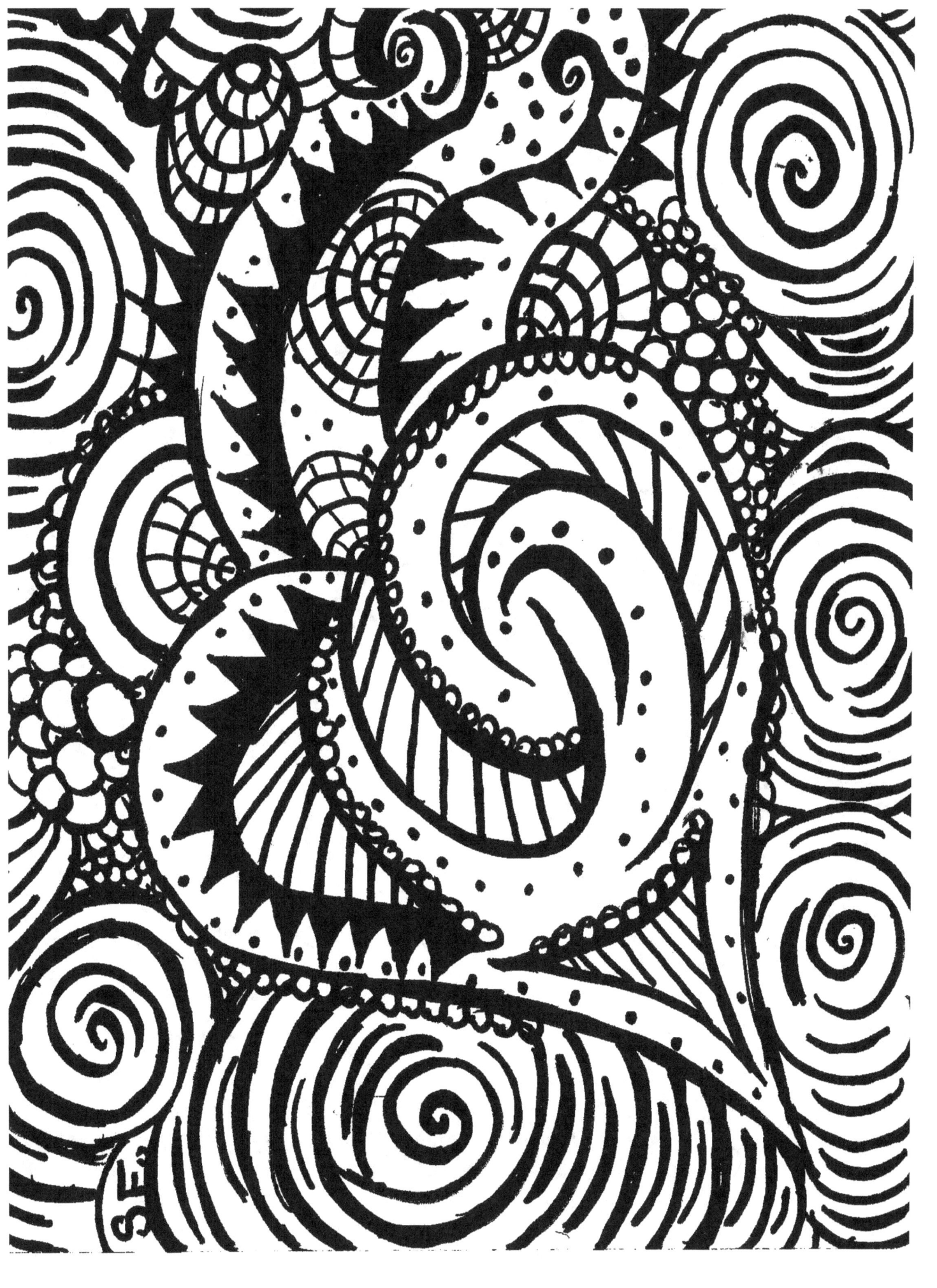

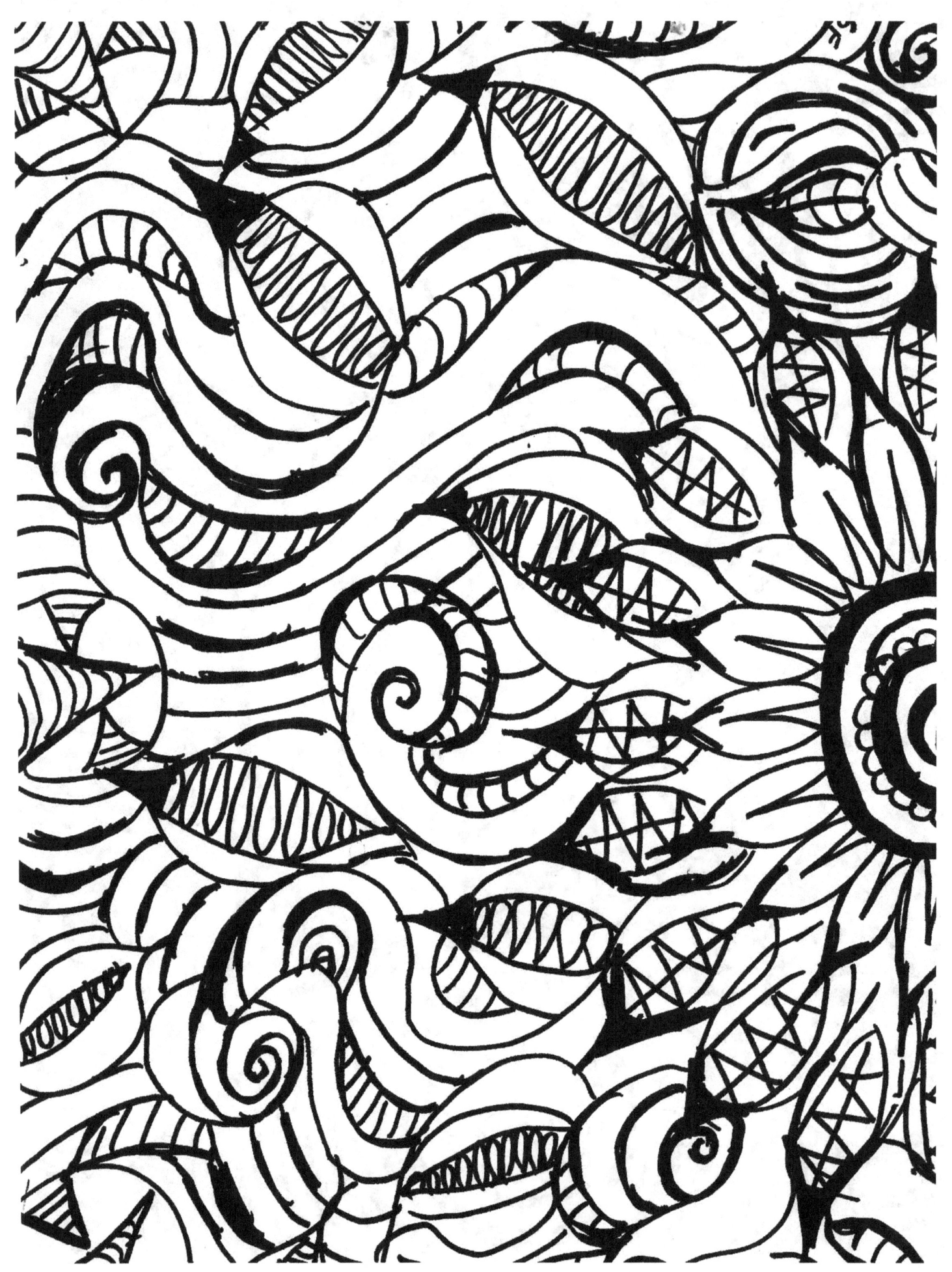

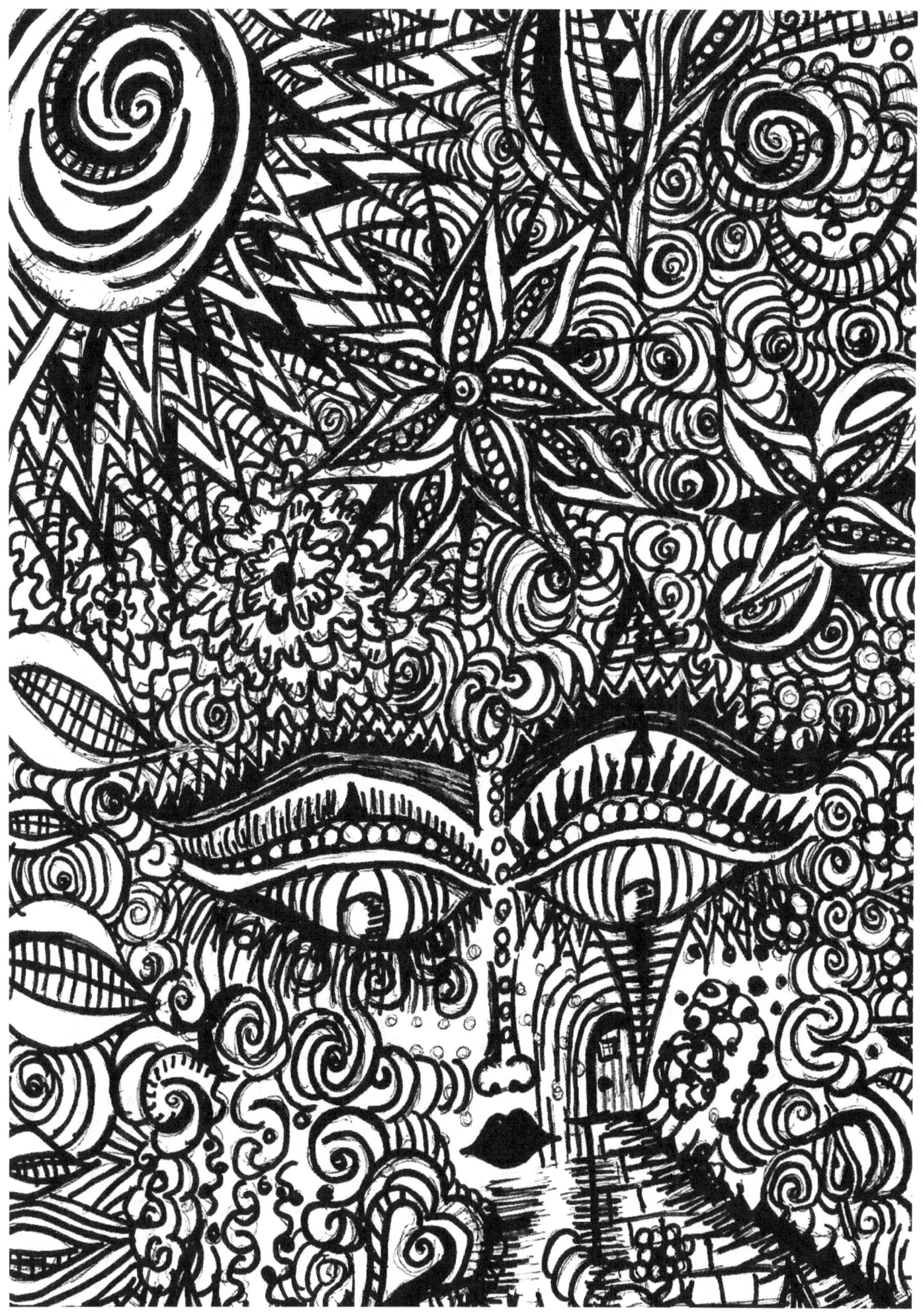

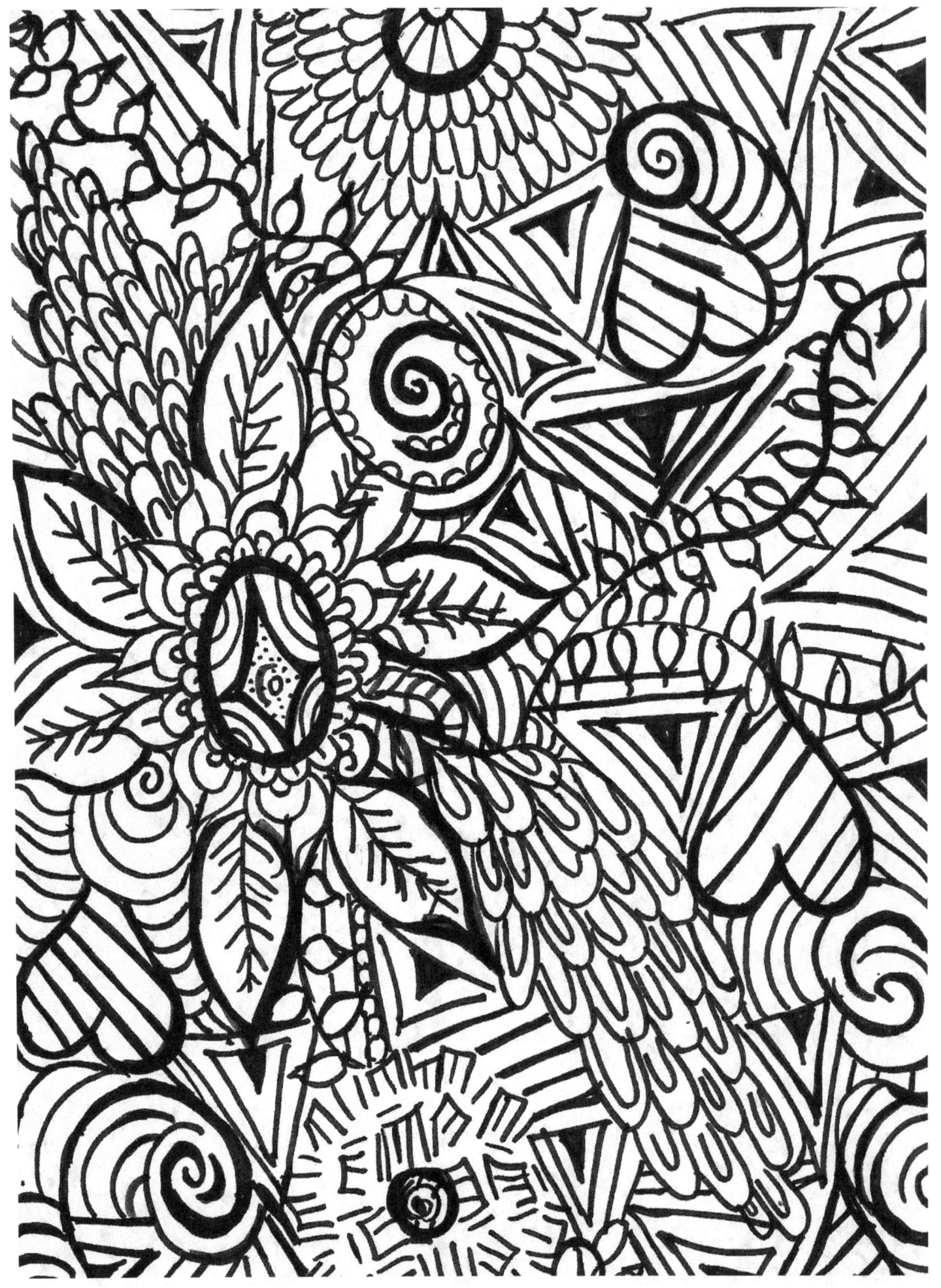

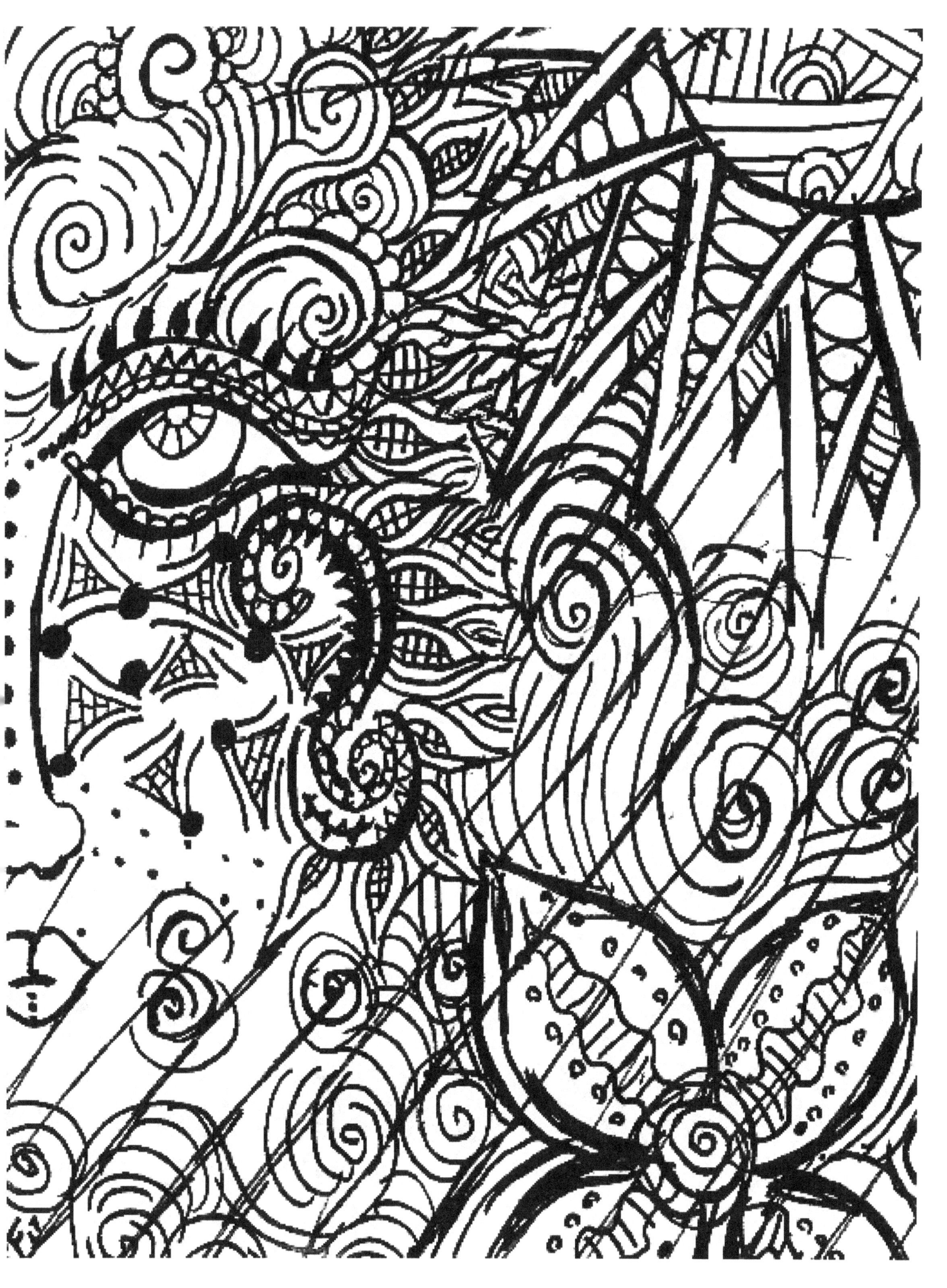

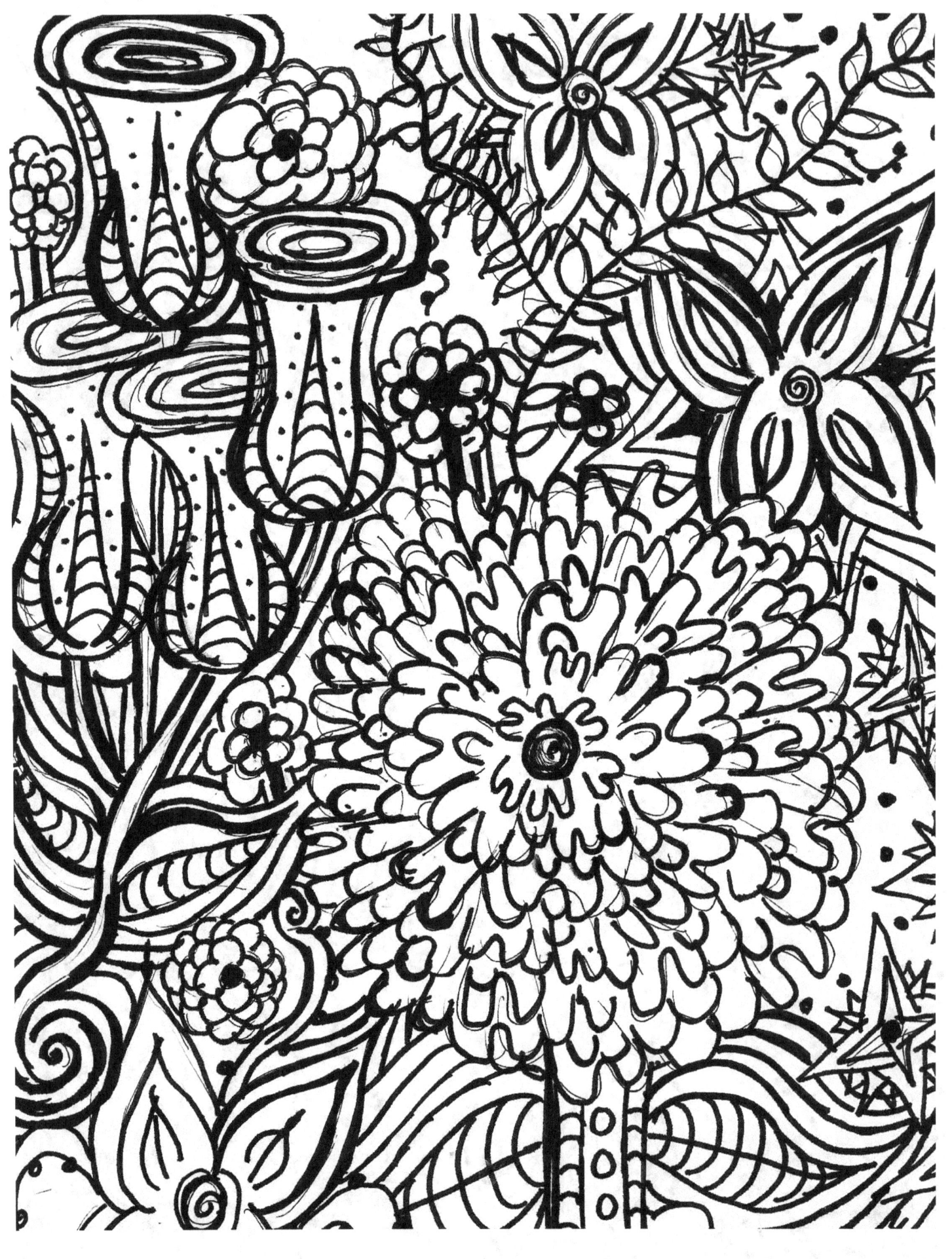

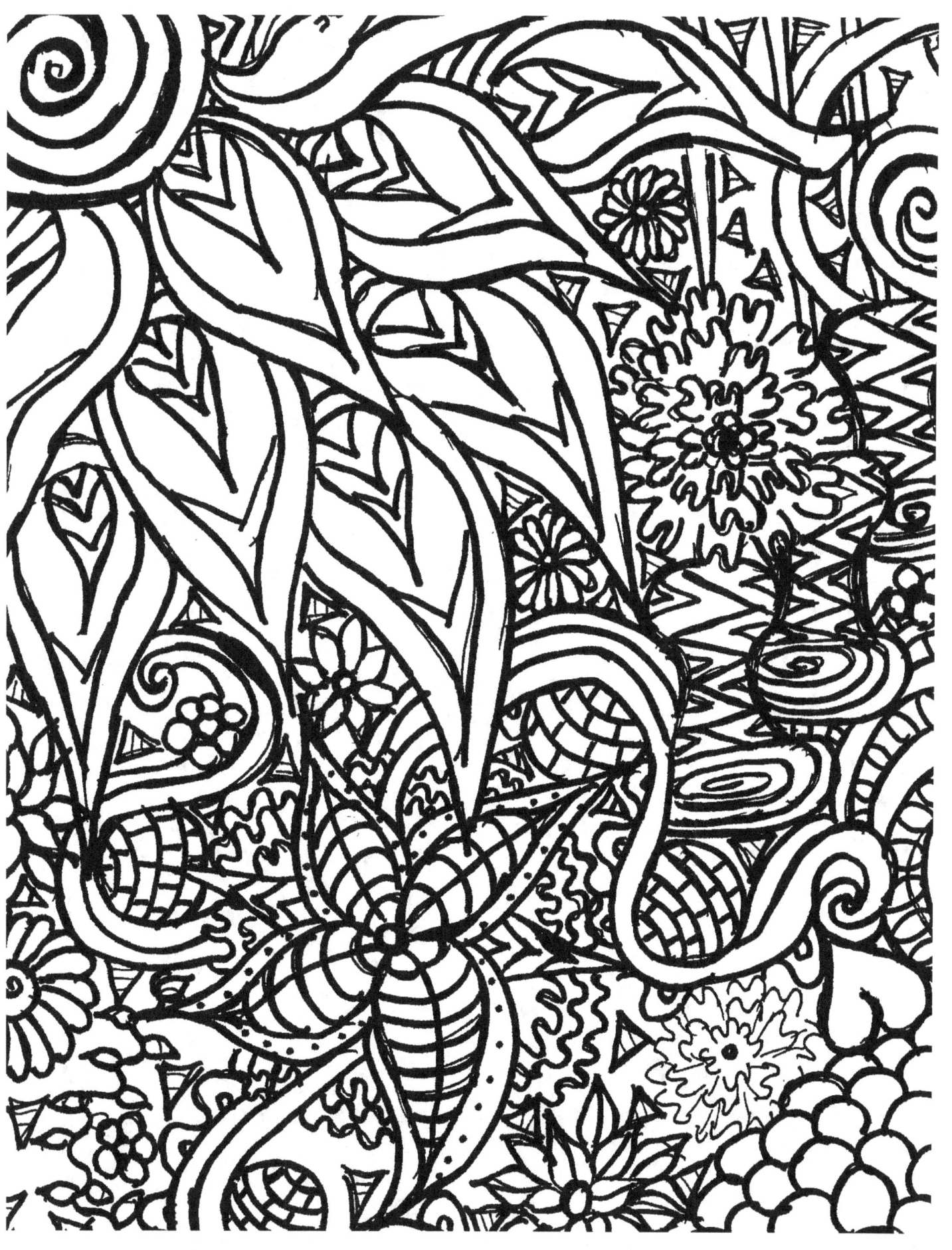

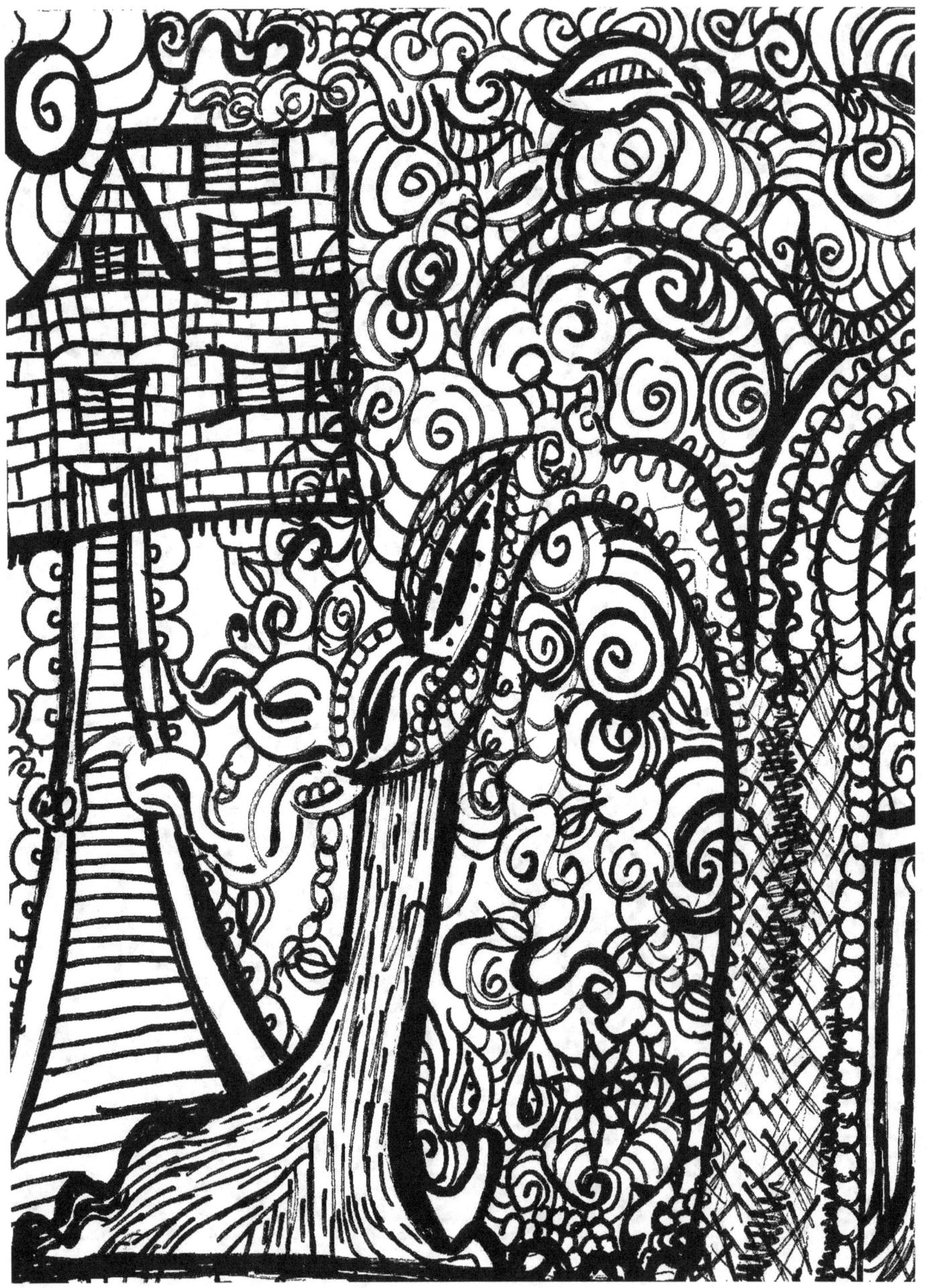

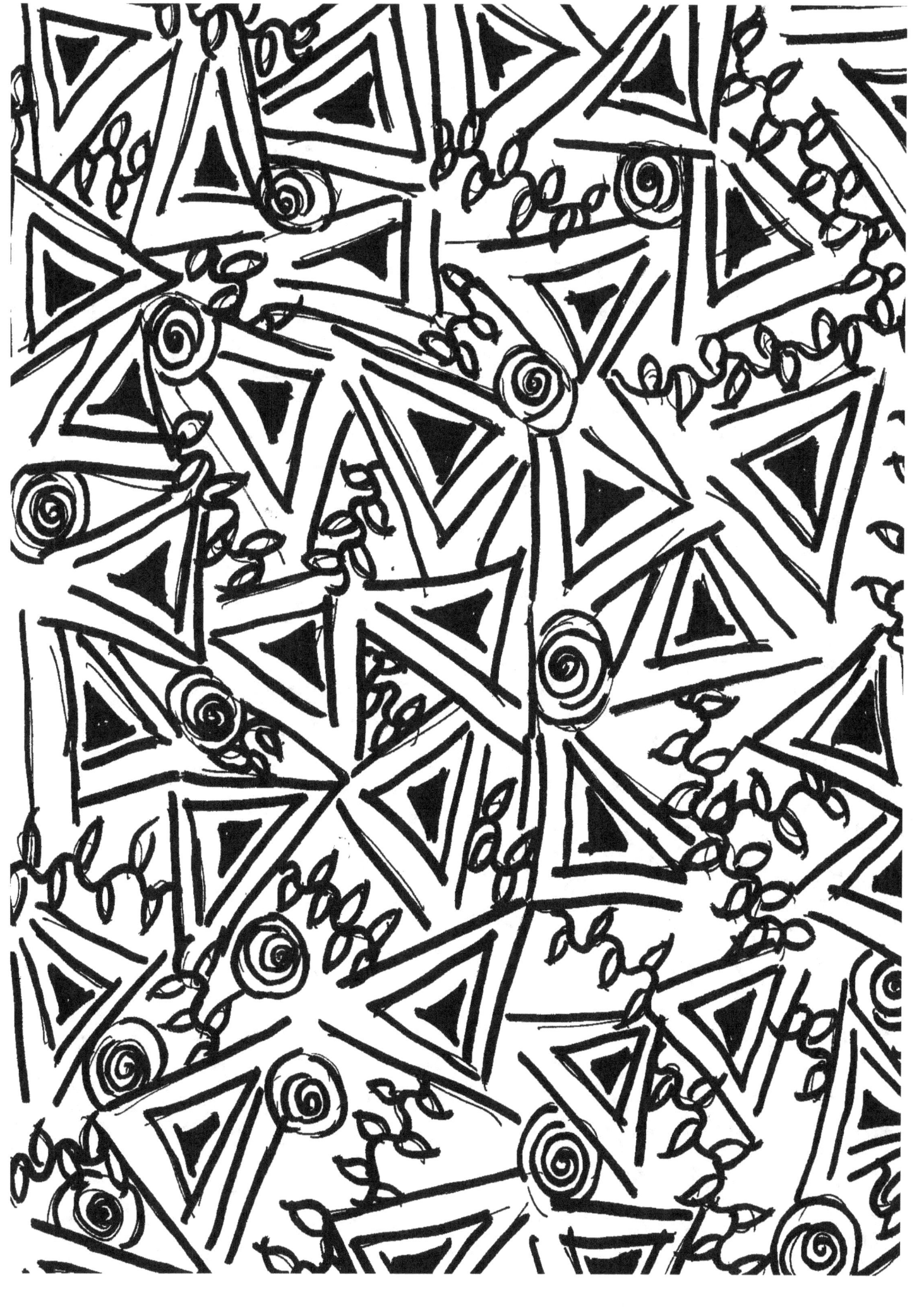

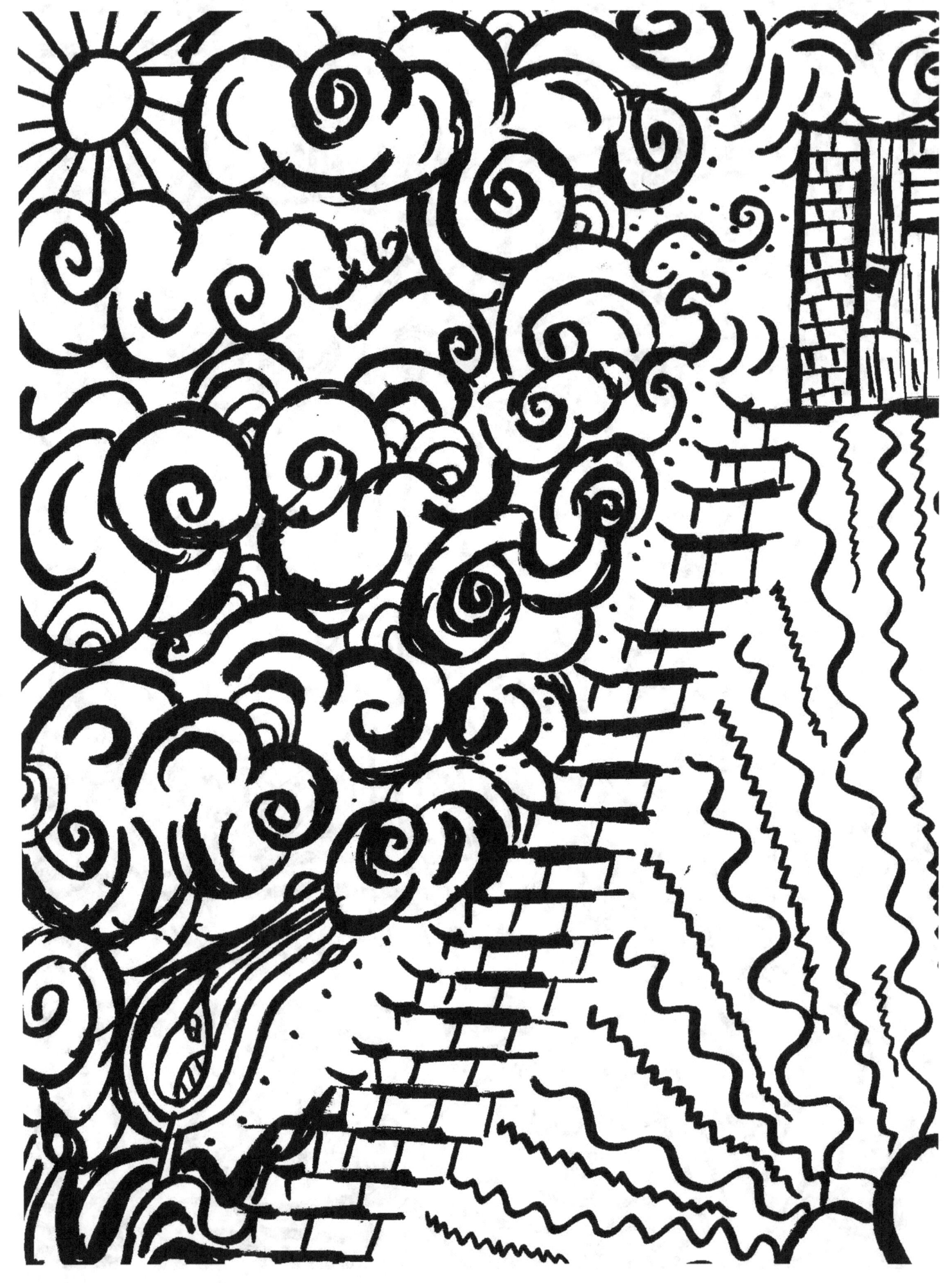

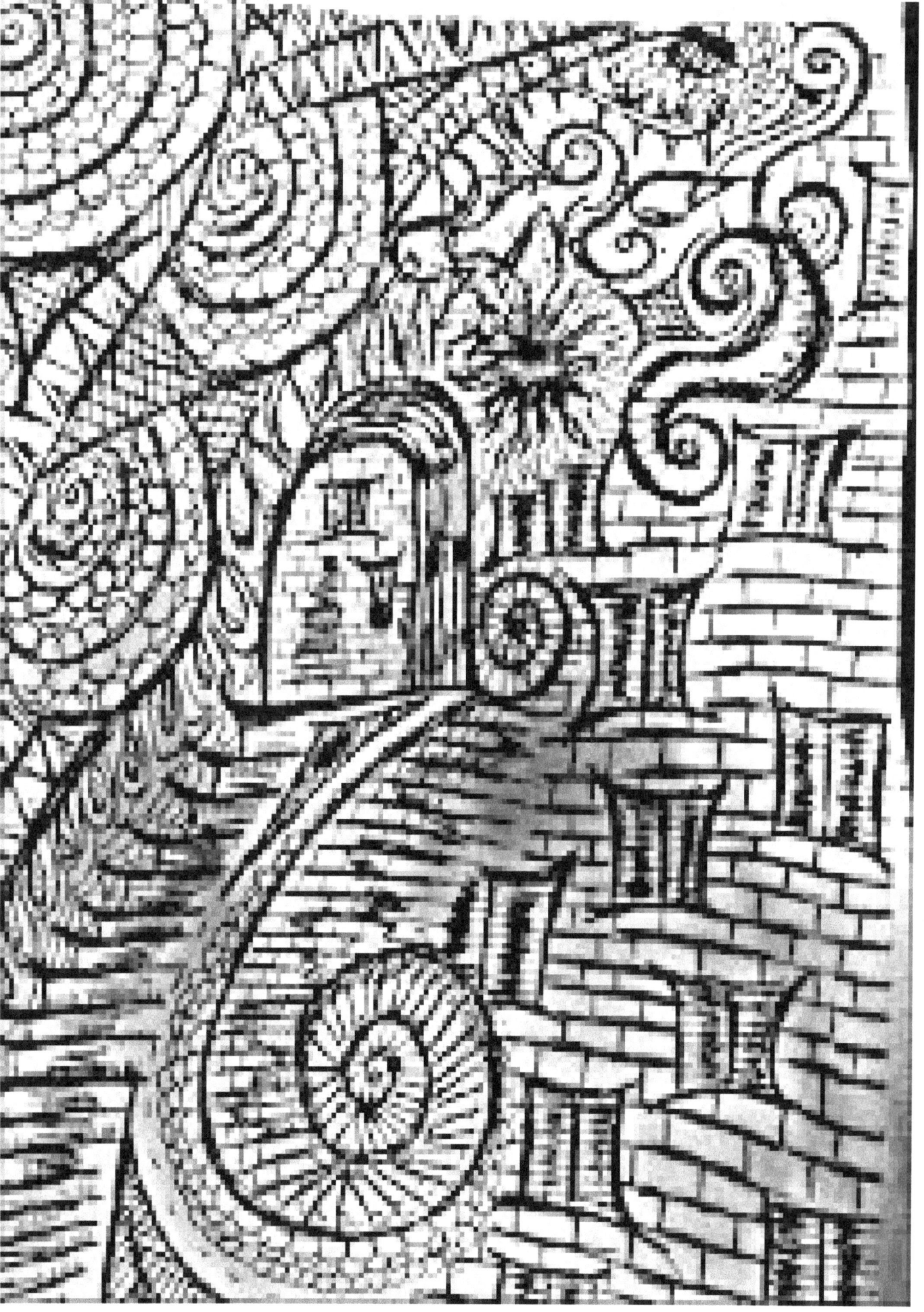

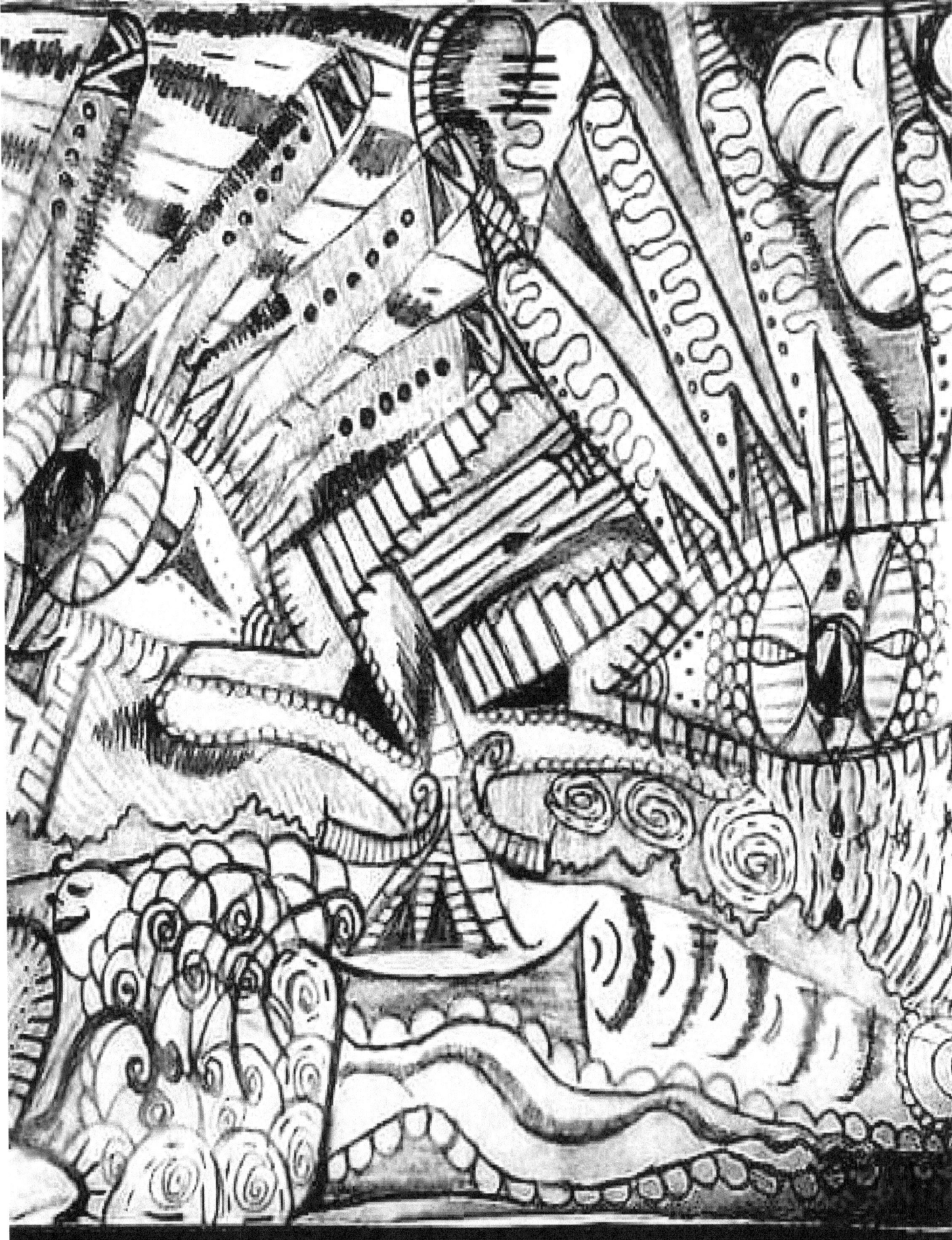

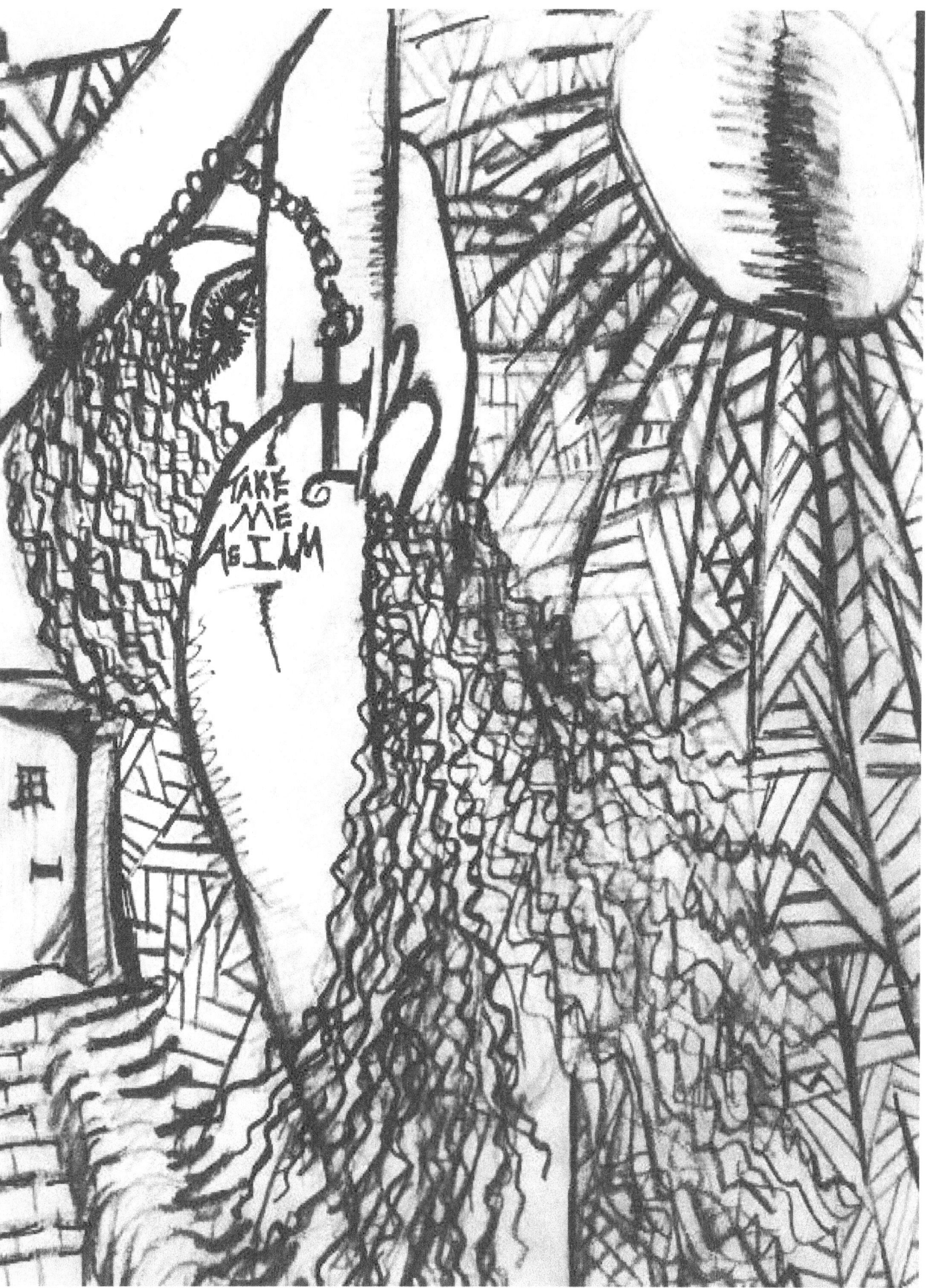

Thanks for your Support

NOTE:
2 more COLOR THERAPY
books on the way
FOLLOW ME.......

LOOKING FOR A
B+ KIDNEY FOR
shanice figeroux
Msfigeroux28@
gmail.com
BOOK IS FOR
SALE "NOW"
sites
Createspace.com
NOW........and
AMAZON.COM
September 3rd

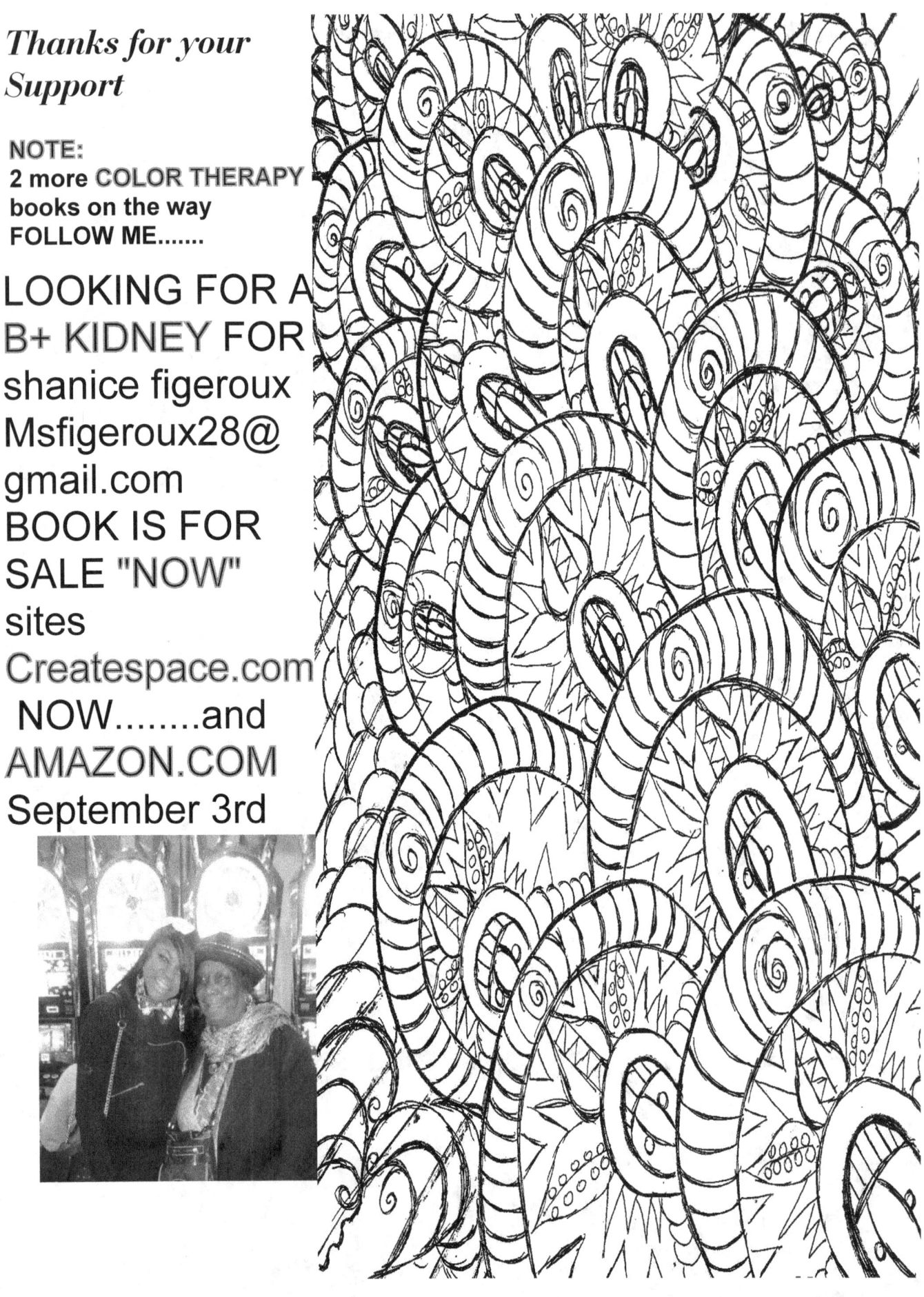